B ARACK OB___ ___ ___ ___ ___ ___ ___ ___ cat out of the b___ when, sh___ ___ ___ Obam_ was elected president, he said, "A crisis is a terrible thing to waste." Washington loves a crisis, because it justifies the existence of bureaucrats, politicians, federal agencies and edicts. Government becomes the savior – even, as now, when government policy mistakes created the crisis in the first place. This is why government in Washington always expands and very rarely recedes during a national security or economic crisis.

So when the stock market crashed by 1,200 points, big banks like Lehman Brothers, Bear Stearns and Citibank teetered on the brink of bankruptcy and the financial system seemed on the verge of a 1929-style collapse, the answer proposed by politicians and bureau-crats was the greatest experiment in big gov-ernment in 50 years.

Did it work? Ask Vice President Joe Biden, and the answer is, it worked, as he put it in September 2009, "beyond my wildest dreams." But for most Americans, this is a nightmare,

[1]

> *Washington loves a crisis, because it justifies the existence of bureaucrats, politicians, federal agencies and edicts.*

not a dream come true. In fact, the $2.8 trillion experiment in government begun tentatively in George W. Bush's last months and continued with arrogant enthusiasm during Obama's first months has been a depressing failure. For all of President Obama's cheery talk of "necessary government intervention to prevent a depression," the statistics tell a demoralizing tale:

> ‣ The dollar stands at only 60 percent of its value in 2007, as our paper currency continues to deteriorate in purchasing power.

> ‣ The U.S. gross domestic product has fallen by a breathtaking 9 percent. Some $7 trillion of wealth had evaporated from the start of the recession through autumn 2009.

› The ranks of the unemployed have increased by 4 million since the September 2008 crash, and all of the job-stimulus bills have only led to higher and higher unemployment, which, at press time, nears 10 percent, its highest rate since 1983 and up from 5 percent before the crisis hit.

› The debt has already widened by $2 trillion, and the hands on the debt clock can barely swirl fast enough to keep pace with the voracious borrowing of the present Congress.

› The Census Bureau reports that personal incomes of Americans, the poverty rate and the wealth of Americans took their worst tumble in two decades – *after* the government fix.

As we stare at these facts through the haze of Obamanomics, we can see certain truths. We know, for instance, that a major trigger point for our depressed economy was too much debt and too much spending that we couldn't afford. Households accumulated too much credit-card and mortgage debt. Businesses took on too much leverage (think of Bear Stearns and Lehman Brothers, with debt-to-asset ratios of more than 30-to-1). And the federal government took on more debt than any other institution on the face of the planet, most of it to finance absurdly wasteful spending. Some of this spending took place under Republicans, as Rep. Nancy Pelosi, Sen. Harry Reid and the rest of the Democrats who now run Congress never tired of telling us when their party did not control the White House. But when Pelosi became speaker of the House, the deficit was $160 billion. It went to $400 billion in one year, and, another year later, the debt reached $1.58 trillion.

So if the Democrats were telling us that all of this excessive debt under Bush caused the economic crisis, how is more debt supposed to get us out of it? The idea of borrowing more and more money today to pay off all the people we borrowed money from in the 1990s

and 2000s is a debt-based Ponzi scheme –
Bernie Madoff economics.

CASH FOR POLICY CLUNKERS

The excruciating history of a year's worth of
relentless policy mistakes can be retold in a
hurry. First came the bailout of Bear Stearns,
the Wall Street investment bank. That cost an
estimated $29 billion – a jaw-dropping figure
at the time that would soon seem like loose
change.

Then came the $400 billion federal bailout
of Fannie Mae and Freddie Mac, the quasi-
governmental home mortgage guarantee
agency. Rep. Barney Frank, the chairman of
the House Financial Services Committee,
had condemned editorials in *The Wall Street
Journal* for calling these agencies houses of
cards with huge and mounting systemic risk.
Frank told us that they didn't need adult
supervision. He even said that when it came
to Fannie Mae, he wanted to "roll the dice."

Uncle Sam did just this, and we all had to pay when the dice crapped out.

But Congress was just getting started. Two weeks later came the AIG insurance company bailout, another $182 billion when all was said and done. But this was just a warm-up for the $700 billion bailout of the banks. The Troubled Asset Relief Program, or TARP, took money from taxpayers and sound banks and handed it over to banks that took on excessive risks with subprime mortgages. Some banks might be in better shape a year later, but we've allowed others that should have failed to keep operating, rewarding bad risks and excessive leveraging and sanctifying a new doctrine in finance called "too big to fail."

Some of the best economists I know believe that the bailout of the banks was absolutely necessary to prevent a collapse of the financial system. They worried that we might have had a domino effect of failing banks without the infusion of tax funds to keep the banks solvent. Perhaps that is true. We did, thankfully, avert a 1930s-style bankruptcy contagion of the banks. One big problem, however, is that the bank-rescue plan has become an excuse in Washington to bail out any large firm that is facing bankruptcy. We now have a de facto "too big to fail" doctrine in Washing-

---

The idea of borrowing more and more money today to pay off all the people we borrowed money from in the 1990s and 2000s is a debt-based Ponzi scheme — Bernie Madoff economics.

---

ton, where nearly every major corporation has an implicit federal taxpayer safety net to protect them from the repercussions of their bad business decisions or their financial gambles that don't pay off.

As the Obama administration took power, White House Chief of Staff Rahm Emanuel, embellishing on his comment about not wasting a crisis, told a liberal audience that they could, in fact, use the financial crisis to "do things that they normally could not do." And President Obama quickly acted on that insight by asking Congress to enact a $1 trillion spending plan that went to items that had been jotted down on the liberal wish list, without much hope of ever coming to pass, over the previous 40 years.

There would be money for the National Endowment for the Arts, for Head Start, for unemployment insurance, for renewable energy subsidies, for a new fleet of cars for bureaucrats. There would be a bailout of the pork industry (how appropriate!), tens of billions for new labor union jobs and housing aid that would be ciphered through corrupt left-wing "welfare lobby groups," like ACORN (Association of Community Organizations for Reform Now).

This was supposed to result in "shovel-ready infrastructure," like roads, bridges and school construction. But only 15 percent of the money was for such brick-and-mortar projects. Most of the rest of the money lined the pockets of the groups that made the 2008 election possible. Even Congress, though, couldn't stomach a $1 trillion program when the budget deficit was already headed to $1 trillion – nearly double the all-time record. So the price tag was shaved to $800 billion and passed with pompous pronouncements about how the public weal had been served.

The president noted that amid this spending free-for-all, families would be getting tax-rebate checks of $500 to $1,000 to help make ends meet. What a deal, responded Brian Riedl, budget expert of The Heritage Foundation. Tax cuts of $1,000 for a family, but $13,000 in new debt.

The Obama budget is filled with more than three dozen tax credits and new spending programs allegedly designed to help stretch the incomes of middle-class families – including Obama's signature tax cut of a $400 credit per household. But to get the $400 tax credit, each family in America will have to bear nearly $100,000 of its share of the new debt on the federal credit card. No wonder so many Americans have come to recognize the Obama giveaways as a kind of fool's gold!

But the Obama administration was just getting started. A few weeks after the stimulus came the president's new 10-year budget blueprint, a decadelong socialist fantasy that read as though ghostwritten by Hugo Chávez. It called for $40 trillion of government spending over the next decade, financed by tax hikes on the rich (more about that later) and an ungodly level of new debt, projected at $9 trillion – which surely was an underestimate. Under Obamanomics, the government would borrow more money in 10 years than it had in the first 225 years.

GOVERNMENT MOTORS

The Obama administration wasn't finished completing the nationalization of industry that began with banks, mortgage companies, insurance firms and Wall Street investment houses. Next on the debt assembly line was a multibillion-dollar takeover of the auto industry allegedly designed to save Chrysler and General Motors but actually created to rescue the United Auto Workers. With a potential price tag of $100 billion for the two companies, it would have been cheaper for taxpayers to write a $300,000 check for every autoworker at GM and Chrysler in return for their promise never to make another car.

In the unconstitutional bankruptcy that was designed by shrewd UAW lawyers and the White House, the federal government essentially stole $3 billion to $5 billion from the companies, which was rightfully owned by the GM and Chrysler creditors, and reassigned the money to the unions. This overrode hundreds of years of corporate contract law that says creditors are first in line – before stock owners, workers and other stakeholders – to claim the assets of a company. The Obama administration ripped up those creditors' contracts and strong-armed the bondholders to take pennies on the dollars they were owed. Lost in the shuffle was an obvious and enduring truth: America is a rich nation, after all, precisely because we believe in the sanctity of contracts and property rights.

GM and Chrysler emerged from a trumped-up bankruptcy owned jointly by the United States government, the Canadian government and the autoworkers union. Given the congenital incapacity of government to run enterprises at a profit, the likely result is that U.S. taxpayers will be shoveling tens of billions of dollars into these car companies year after year until Government Motors finally goes out of business. Think Amtrak.

An even more unprecedented seizure of power was the Fed's decision to buy up failing assets in the U.S. – especially subprime mortgages. The Fed more than doubled the assets it holds on its balance sheet, from $1 trillion to roughly $2 trillion. The collateral standing behind thousands of these mortgage-backed securities are subprime homes that have already been defaulted or foreclosed on. They are junk-quality bonds, bought by taxpayers to further bail out banks and homeowners.

The Fed even began to buy up hundreds of billions of dollars of treasury securities. As the Treasury was issuing debt, the Fed was buying it up – by printing more money.

A Debtfare State

It is hard to believe today that in 2006, when Democrats took over Congress, Pelosi stated, "Democrats are committed to no deficit spending. We will not heap mountains of debt onto future generations."

It wasn't hard to claim the mantle of fiscal responsibility back then, because the Republicans had created half-trillion-dollar deficits. So in 2006 and 2007, Pelosi preached to us from the Gospel According to St. Robert Rubin that the Bush budget deficits are evil and immoral and driving up interest rates; we need to atone for those sins by repealing the Bush tax cuts; and we must install pay-as-you-go budgeting so big deficits never happen again.

But once they took power and the economy

wavered, the Democrats discovered the irrelevance of fiscal discipline. No lesser an authority than Rubin himself declared in early September 2009 that deficits aren't so bad after all: "Fiscal stimulus can give the economy a timely boost in the face of great uncertainty and concern with the short-term economic outlook." In other words, go out and run up the federal credit card, and you can still feel good about yourself in the morning, although there will ultimately come a morning that is the morning after.

As the current recession has worsened, Congress and then Obama have kept bidding up the price of a stimulus. First, it was $40 billion. Then Secretary of State Hillary Clinton said $60 billion. On the eve of the financial meltdown, Pelosi was talking $100 billion. Then Obama proposed his $1 trillion spending bomb. But the Congressional Budget Office forecast was that we were already scheduled to borrow $1 trillion in 2009 – without any further stimulus. This was already twice as much borrowing as in any year since World War II.

A few weeks later, the Obama budget was delivered into our laps. That budget increases government spending by $817 billion over the next five years, and those numbers are lowball estimates. The debt grows by more than $1 trillion a year for the next five years, settling at $11.5 trillion in 2013. Over the decade, the debt rises by $9 trillion. It creates major new entitlements for health care, welfare and unemployment benefits that could blow another $2 trillion hole in the already $50 trillion unfunded liabilities crisis. The roughly 8,000 domestic agencies of government receive a $50.9 billion budget hike. That's a 9.3 percent spending hike over last year, which is spectacularly generous, given that many federal agencies already received more than 70 percent increases in their budgets, thanks to the $800 billion stimulus plan passed earlier this year. The president also proposed a $150 billion line of credit for new foreign aid programs, almost three times more than ever spent.

Yet only a few days after this budget was released, the president promised a return to "fiscal responsibility." He told the country that his agenda of bailouts, budget deficits, and runaway spending is motivated "not because I believe in bigger government – I don't." You could have fooled me.

In the Ronald Reagan, George H. W. Bush and Bill Clinton years, when Democrats wanted to raise taxes, they argued that the deficit must be brought down to lower interest rates. But now they propose to raise the deficit exponentially, exposing the deficit phobia of the Rubin wing of the Democratic party as a hypocritical ruse for Democrats to pay homage to "fiscal responsibility" when Republicans want to cut tax rates to grow the economy. When Democrats want to grow government spending, deficits don't matter so much after all – even when they are in the trillions of dollars.

In a public-relations ploy to pretend to prove that the president really does want a "new era of fiscal responsibility," the Obama budget office scrubbed line by line through the budget to find waste, fraud and abuse. It discovered $16.7 billion of budget savings by cutting 121 programs. This is about how much the feds spend every three days, or, to be more exact, 0.45 cents of savings out of every dollar Uncle Sam will spend this year.

By all means, get rid of the Denali job training program (savings: $3 million), USDA public broadcasting grants (savings: $5 million), and payments to high-income farmers (savings: $58 million). But compared with the moonshot approach needed to deal with debt, this was a bottle rocket. Three-quarters of the budget savings come from the national defense budget, not from domestic agencies. Of the 10-year savings of $71 billion in entitlement programs – which are now a mind-numbing $62.9 trillion in debt over the long-term – one-third of the cutbacks are not cuts at all: They are tax increases, mostly on the oil and gas industries.

This left $4.7 billion of cuts from programs like agriculture subsidies and Medicare, which sounds like a lot, but at the very moment Obama was announcing these cuts, the Democrats in the Senate were pushing forward a new universal health-care program that will add between $1 trillion and $1.5 trillion of *new* unfunded costs over those same 10 years.

It's hard to take $17 billion of savings seriously when the government spent more than 10 times that much money to bail out one company, AIG. At the pace Obama is setting, with $16.7 billion of savings a year and assuming no new debt, the budget will be balanced by around 2110.

The Obama administration and congressional Democrats defend their record deficits and debt by pointing the finger at Bush. And, in fact, spending in the eight years before Obama came to power expanded from $1.789 trillion in 2000 to $2.979 trillion in 2008. That's a 67 percent increase. How many Americans saw *their* incomes grow by 67 percent? Quick, raise your hand.

Now that they are in power, the Democrats

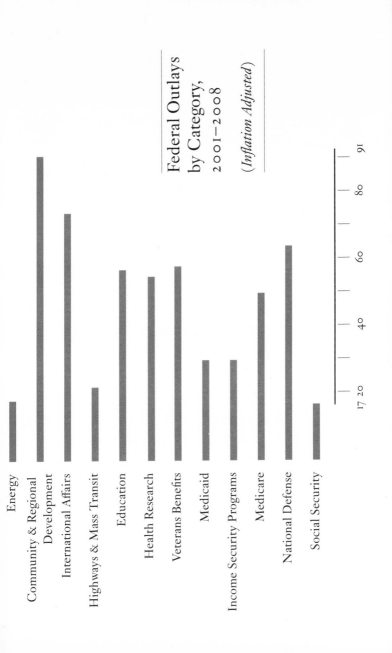

Federal Outlays
by Category,
2001–2008

(*Inflation Adjusted*)

Energy

Community & Regional
Development

International Affairs

Highways & Mass Transit

Education

Health Research

Veterans Benefits

Medicaid

Income Security Programs

Medicare

National Defense

Social Security

17 20   40   60   80   91

claim that the spendthrift Bush years were pinched and niggardly, intentionally starving vital infrastructure and social services. But this idea is confounded by the chart below, which compares government spending with the major areas of "investment" that liberals insist need more funding. Most of these areas grew during the Bush presidency by four, five or six times the rate of inflation.

In Obama's first half-year in office, these budgets rose another 54 percent – or 30 times the rate of inflation – according to the House Committee on the Budget.

The Soak-the-Rich Fallacy

High tax rates are a staple of the Obama agenda. As the president has put it, the people who made money in the past two decades of Bush-enabled greed should pay more to cover the cost of health care, unemployment insurance, foreign aid and bridges to nowhere.

The tax increases he has proposed would bring tax rates on the productive and job-creating class in America to their highest levels since the 1970s. Obama would raise the capital gains tax rate to 20 percent from the current 15 percent, the dividend tax to the 20–28 percent range from 15 percent and the income-tax rate to 39.6 percent from 35 percent. But he also wants an income-tax surcharge on the richest group of 5 percent to raise the top rate to nearly 45 percent. The president has said that he also wants to raise the payroll tax on those with incomes over $250,000 by 2 to 4 percentage points. Combined, this would raise the highest tax rate to the 45–50 percent range. The table on page 22 shows the impact of all of these tax rate hikes.

Since roughly two out of three of tax filers who fall into this income category are small-business owners, operators or investors, these taxes are aimed straight at the balance sheet of the American entrepreneur and job creator. Can higher tax liabilities entice this group to hire more workers? (It's worth noting that in the first four years that Bush cut these tax

Obama Tax Plan

	Current	Obama Proposal
Income-Tax Rate	35%	45–50%
Combined Income/ Payroll	37.4%	49–54%
Capital Gains	15%	20%
Dividends	15%	20–28%
Estate Tax (2010)	0%	55%
Payroll Tax	15%	23%*

* For employers without health insurance.

rates, tax payments by Americans with an income of more than $1 million doubled, and jobs increased by 8 million.)

There is another problem with the notion that soaking the rich will balance the budget. Even if the federal government were to take every penny from those who are in the richest 1 percent of income, this would only yield a little less than $2 trillion. That is what the government spends in eight months. So even a 100 percent tax wouldn't raise enough. The Congressional Budget Office says that tax rates would have to rise to 75 percent or 80 percent to balance the budget in the coming years. Even many liberals agree that tax rates that high would destroy the U.S. economy.

Barack Obama, Meet Christina Romer

One person whose research shows that higher taxes can be chaotic and destructive is Christina Romer, the president's chief economic adviser. Here is what she said about taxes, back when she was teaching at the University of California, Berkeley: "Tax increases appear to have a very large, sustained and highly significant negative impact on output."

Romer and her husband, David Romer, who were professors of economics at the University of California, Berkeley, wrote this in an exhaustive 2009 study on U.S. tax policy changes over the past 100 years. The Obama economics team should pay closer attention to one of its own. Christina Romer's findings are a tutorial on why raising tax rates, especially during a time of economic crisis, can be highly destructive.

Perhaps most relevant to the current economic policy debate is Romer's analysis of the Herbert Hoover income-tax-rate increases at

---

If you want a growing economy, more investment, more jobs and a lower deficit, cut tax rates, don't raise them.

---

the start of the Great Depression. She writes, "The revenue act of 1932 increased American tax rates greatly in an attempt to balance the budget, and by doing so dealt another contractionary blow to the economy. . . ." Repeating that mistake would be a grievous error.

Raising tax rates for the rich is simply a futile way to raise government revenues. Back in 1980, when the top tax rate was 70 percent, the richest 1 percent paid 19 percent of all income taxes. Today, with a top tax rate of 35 percent, the richest 1 percent pay 40.1 percent of income taxes. Cutting the tax rate in half *doubled* the tax contribution from the rich. If you want a growing economy, more investment, more jobs and a lower deficit, cut tax rates, don't raise them.

Even liberal think tanks agree that taxing the rich will get about $32 billion a year in new revenues. But the budget deficit is $1.58 trillion. Where will the other $1.55 trillion come from? This brings us to the greatest myth of all, that 95 percent of Americans will be spared the agony of tax cuts. It was Obama's most memorable promise. But now, Democrats are starting to see they can't pay for all their spending and get the money from the richest 1 percent, 2 percent or even 5 percent of our citizens. So, for example, the $1 trillion health-care reform bill includes seven new taxes on the middle class, including a $3,000 income-tax penalty on working families who don't purchase health insurance.

After just nine months in office and the wildest spending binge in history —already $3.4 trillion of new federal spending has been enacted or proposed for the next decade – the Obama administration concluded that for the government to pay its bills, taxes are going to have go up – way up. And not just on the richest 1 percent, 2 percent or 5 percent, but on everyone – not with an income above $250,000, but above $2,500.

It's not hard to figure out how they've come to this conclusion. The Chinese, among others, have warned that Obama's $10 trillion of deficits over the next decade could upend the entire world financial system. But this White House isn't remotely interested in cutting spending. Its top priority is to hatch a new 10-year, $1 trillion health-care charge when the existing health-care programs are already $30 trillion in debt.

No responsible economist believes the Obama fairy tale, that this deficit can be brought down substantially by taxing the rich. It is the middle class, which the president admits is living paycheck-to-paycheck in this recession, that will ultimately have the privilege of paying for his administration's unpaid bills for an $880 billion stimulus plan, $200 billion in industry bailouts, the trillion-dollar health-care expansions, and hundreds of billions for renewable energy subsidies.

Brace yourself, because this gets expensive. First comes the 10–15 percent payroll tax on workers without health care to pay for Obama-Care. That's about $5,000 for a middle-class

---

No responsible economist believes the Obama fairy tale, that this deficit can be brought down substantially by taxing the rich.

---

family. Next is the $850 billion cap-and-trade legislation energy tax which, if passed by the Senate, will be paid by rich and poor alike through higher gasoline and utility bills. This will raise average family utility and gas taxes by about $500 per year.

Finally, there is the specter of the tax the American left has secretly coveted for decades: a European-style national sales tax, or value-added tax (VAT). A 5 percent national sales tax would be a cash cow for Uncle Sam, raising $250 billion to $500 billion a year, depending on exemptions. This is, of course, a highly regressive tax and blows to smithereens once and for all the idea that the middle class gets a net tax cut under Obama. (The experience of Europe is that VATs have not lowered budget deficits but instead have given politicians money to underwrite the socialists' cradle-to-grave welfare state expansions.)

The Democrats have long wanted to install a Swedish-style gold-plated welfare state in America, and all that has been missing is the Swedish-style tax on families to pay for it. To get from here to there the left will have to tax the middle class, as the Europeans do, because, as Willie Sutton famously replied when asked why he robbed banks) "That is where the money is." So thanks to the $9 trillion of debt spending that we have in the pipeline, one thing is certain about paying for Obamanomics: Taxes are going up not just for the rich scapegoats, but for everyone.

THE ROAD FROM SERFDOM

We are in the midst of one of the great ideological battles in the history of America. The left has seized on an economic crisis, largely created by its own money machine programs, to vastly expand government power well beyond anything before seen in America. It is no exaggeration to say that we will not recognize our country in 10 years if all of the spending, the cap-and-trade climate-change measures, the government takeover of the health-care system, the higher tax rates and the spectacular debt bubble endure.

We have become one nation with two wholly divergent views of how to grow a prospering economy that lifts all boats. No wonder there are massive protests among Americans all over the country marching against a not-so-slow road to socialism and tyranny.

George Washington warned against what we now face when he said, "Government is . . . a fearsome master." Ronald Reagan, godfather of the alternative vision of low taxes, limited government and individual freedom to choose, put it another way: "A government big enough to give you everything you want is big enough to take everything you've got."

At times like this, I become more nostalgic for the indispensable missing voice in this debate: Milton Friedman's. No one could slice and dice the sophistry of the left's government-market interventions better than Friedman. Imagine what he would have to say about the arrogance of the U.S. government owning and operating the car companies or managing the $2 trillion health-care industry. "Why not?" I can almost hear him ask. "After all, they've done such a wonderful job delivering the mail." (USPS, by the way, just posted a $4 billion loss, even as service deteriorates. And these are the people we are going to allow to run our health-care system?)

I've been thinking a lot lately about one of my last conversations with Friedman, when he warned that "even though socialism is a discredited economic model and capitalism is raising living standards to new heights, the left intellectuals continue to push for bigger government everywhere I look." He predicted that people would be seduced by collectivist ideas again. He was right.

In the midst of this global depression, not only are rotten ideas all the rage, like trillion-dollar Keynesian stimulus plans, nationalization of banks, a government takeover of the health-care system and confiscatory taxes on America's wealth producers, but Friedman-esque principles of global free trade, low tax rates and deregulation are being accused of murdering global prosperity. When The University of Chicago wanted to create a $200 million Milton Friedman Institute, Sen. Bernie Sanders of Vermont, a proud and self-admitted socialist, snarled that the university must never "align itself with a reactionary political program supported by the wealthiest, greediest and most powerful people and institutions in this country." Then he finished his rant by fuming, "Friedman's ideology caused enormous damage to the American middle class and to working families here and around the world."

The indisputable truth is just the opposite, of course. Prof. Andrei Shleifer, who has written a just-in-time tribute in the prestigious *Journal of Economic Literature* aptly titled "The Age of Milton Friedman," writes, "The last quarter-century [from 1980 to 2005] has witnessed remarkable progress of mankind. As the world embraced free market policies, living standards rose sharply while life expectancy, educational attainment, and democracy improved and absolute poverty declined." He documents that Deng Xiaoping in China, Margaret Thatcher of Britain and Reagan in the U.S. led the charge toward free markets, and "all three of these leaders professed inspiration from the work of Milton Friedman."

Even the United Nations recently conceded that, thanks to the expansion of free trade and globalization, the number of people in the world living in abject poverty (less than $1 a day) fell by almost half in the past 25 years. Friedman's ideas on capitalism and freedom, in other words, did more to liberate humankind from poverty than all of the New Deal, Great Society, welfare state and Obama economic stimulus plans stacked on top of each other.

Perhaps the idea of Friedman's that is most in disrepute is deregulation of industries. The Obama administration is convinced that a new era of regulatory shackles on hedge funds, money managers and banks will restore prosperity. One time, I watched a debate between Friedman and James Tobin, the Keynesian Nobel Prize-winning economist from Yale. Friedman recalled traveling to an Asian country in the 1960s and visiting a project where the government was building a canal. Friedman was shocked to see that, instead of modern tractors and earth movers digging the canal, the workers had shovels. He asked why there were so few modern machines, and the bureaucrat responded, "You don't understand, this is a jobs program." Friedman responded,

We are now witnessing, even if we don't quite realize it, a battle for the soul of America.

"Oh, I thought you were trying to build a canal. If it's jobs you want, then you should give these workers spoons, not shovels."

My hunch is that if Friedman were alive today, he would be telling whoever had the wisdom to listen to him that everything our government has done in response to our economic crisis has been exactly the wrong thing to do.

What would Milton Friedman, architect of our past 25 years of prosperity, tell Americans fearful of the dark economic trough in which they now find themselves? I once asked him, if he could make three policy changes to increase economic growth, what would they be? He unhesitatingly replied, "One, promote free trade; two, create a competitive model in education; and three, cut government spending." How much should we cut spending? He said, "As much as possible."

There is a ready answer to liberals who wring their hands at the high passions and raw emotions that dominate the public square today: It's the economy, stupid. We are now witnessing, even if we don't quite realize it, a battle for the soul of America. The stakes are about as high as they have ever been. You can't tax, borrow and inflate your way to prosperity. Government power grabs will not make us freer. And they certainly won't make us any richer. If we don't learn these lessons very soon, our children will be much the poorer for our economic ignorance and selfishness.

First American edition published in 2009 by Encounter Books,
an activity of Encounter for Culture and Education, Inc.,
a nonprofit, tax exempt corporation.
Encounter Books website address: www.encounterbooks.com

Manufactured in the United States and printed on
acid-free paper. The paper used in this publication meets
the minimum requirements of ANSI/NISO z39.48 1992
(R 1997) (*Permanence of Paper*).

FIRST AMERICAN EDITION

LIBRARY OF CONGRESS CATALOGING-IN-PUBLICATION DATA

Moore, Stephen, 1960–
How Barack Obama is bankrupting the U.S. economy /
by Stephen Moore.
p.   cm.
ISBN-13: 978-1-59403-464-0 (pbk. : alk. paper)
ISBN-10: 1-59403-464-8 (pbk. : alk. paper)
1. Financial crises—United States. 2. Finance—Government
policy—United States. 3. Intervention (Federal government)
4. United States—Economic policy—2001-2009. 5. United
States—Economic policy—2009– 6. United States—Economic
conditions—2001-2009. 7. United States—Economic
conditions—2009– I. Title.
HB3722.M66 2009
330.973—dc22
2009038893

10 9 8 7 6 5 4 3 2 1